WHAT IF GOD ISN'T WHO YOU THINK HE IS, AND NEITHER ARE YOU

Welcome!

Greetings! We're very excited you're going through *The Cure* study guide together!

(First things first. Look around the group and give that knowing look to the one you think might best be the narrator as you go through this study guide. If you have a radio announcer or movie voice-over talent in the group, they'd be a good pick. Or you can just trade off as you feel led, but these pieces should all be read *out loud* in their entirety.)

Just so you get a sense of where we're going-each study session contains:

1) DVD Clips: "Cinema"
2) Group Discussion: "Group"
3) Biblical Reflection: "Taking Off the Filter"
4) Application: "Trying This On"
5) During the Week (by yourself) Reflections: "Settling Convictions"

We're anticipating you've already read this chapter "Two Roads" in *The Cure* book *before* going through each study guide chapter as a group. (If you haven't done this, just bluff for this first session; smile a lot and nod your head like you understand what they're talking about. Or feign an illness. Get up and run out of the room, returning next week fully caught up.)

Directions to Help Your Group Some introductory directions might help on this journey, especially if you're the facilitator for this group.

Goals for the Group
We have some goals for you to experience personally and as a group:

1. First, grasp the answer to the big question of *The Cure*: *What if God is not who you think He is . . . and neither are you?* It's exhilarating to discover or re-discover God's Original Good News!

2. Second, increasingly experience "Living out of who God says I am." This will blanket your life in freedom!

3. Third, experience new levels of authenticity with others in safe communities of trusted love. This is high on God's "to do" list for us. He paid everything for us to experience this life. It changes everything!

GOALS FOR THE GROUP

GUIDELINES TO HELP YOUR GROUP

1. *Cinema*
Start by watching the clips. We think, over the sessions, they paint an incredible growing picture of these truths and this way of life from many generations, ethnicities, genders, and cultural backgrounds. Give yourself some time to reflect on the worldview they begin to create for you. We'll have a question or two for you to help direct this time.

2. *Group*
Move into the group discussion questions. These focus on taking us deeper into the particular chapter of the book. Don't expect everyone to answer every question, or you'll still be in the session when America converts to the metric system!

3. *Taking Off the Filter*
Consider one relevant verse together. This is a hugely important part of our times together. We want to learn to discern how the same scripture would usually be taught very differently in *The Room of Grace* than in *The Room of Good Intentions.* God speaks in one voice, but many of us have added another. This scripture study will hopefully start to form a way of seeing that takes off the distorted filter of "sin-management" theology.

4. *Trying This On*
Conclude group time with an application question to personalize a main concept of the chapter.

5. *Settling Convictions*
Finally, we'll offer concepts and ideas to consider by yourself during the week.

OPTIONS FOR YOUR GROUP

1. We're aware each group will vary in size and available time. Take great freedom to make this fit your setting. Whatever can't be done in this meeting can be finished in whatever ways make the best sense to you. You might want to slow it down and add some additional times together. You may even want to go through the study again a few months later, after new discoveries have set in.

2. Included at the end of each chapter in *The Cure* book are Quick Response barcodes (these will appear as links if you read the book in an electronic format.) These are incredibly helpful Biblical endnotes, videos from the co-authors answering Frequently Asked Questions, stories, and even group exercises or tools, to try out after you've gone through this study. For further study, clarity and expanding this worldview, we've included hours of additional Biblical and relational teaching from all three of us. Found in these same links. You can go through these on your own at anytime. But if the group has the availability to continue meeting, these will form an invaluable ongoing teaching to help create a way of seeing—spanning across every area of our lives. This will help to expand this life in *The Room of Grace*!

3. We hope you won't see *The Cure* guide as simply "another study to make your way through" where participants dole out the *appropriate* religious answer to group questions. Please don't do that. This can be a life-altering experience. This is not merely a 7-week study but an introduction into a *way of life.* There are no expected answers anyone needs to give. This is an opportunity for a group to learn this way of life together. We hope you'll give yourself this great gift. Here we go!

John, Bruce and Bill

CHAPTER
ONE
TWO
ROADS

PART 1: CINEMA

After watching the "Two Roads" clips, take a few minutes to discuss these questions:

1. What do you imagine to be the hope offered in "The Cure"?

2. Why are so many stuck in *The Room of Good Intentions* or on the wayside of *Cynical Disillusionment*?

PART 2: GROUP

By now you've been introduced to life in three pretty distinct realities. *The Room of Good Intentions*, *The Path of Cynical Disillusionment* and *The Room of Grace*.

1. Allow anyone who wants to call out some adjectives to describe what you imagine life is like in *The Room of Good Intentions*.

2. Now do the same for *The Path of Cynical Disillusionment*. What words describe what it feels like to be there?

3. Then do the same for *The Room of Grace*. What words describe what it would feel like there?

Now, several of you take an opportunity to answer these next two questions:

1. If *The Room of Good Intentions* is characterized by what you've described above, why would anyone choose to stay there?

2. Where have you experienced *The Room of Grace* as you've described it?

"The Law makes rebels of people who want to love and be loved."

"The real trick is to allow the desires of the new heart to come out and have a run of the joint."

PART 3: TAKING OFF THE FILTER

Here is that hugely important section where we want to slow down and ponder how we've seen the scriptures, depending upon which room we've been living in. We're convinced many of us have been taught to read the scriptures with man-imposed filters that have prejudiced and distorted the meaning of God's truth. We believe it's critical for us to understand that how we see God and ourselves powerfully affects how we interpret passages. These biblical reflections are meant as only a starting point. You'll learn to do this with all of the scriptures as a way of life; the verses that may have tripped you up, confused you, frightened you or beaten you down. Hopefully we'll eventually get to see all of scripture without the crippling filter that shame and man-made religion has introduced.

Your point of view will control what you see and hear from God's Word. If you are standing in *The Room of Good Intentions*, you will see the same words of the Bible from a different angle than in *The Room of Grace*. There is an entire world of difference between attempting to obey scripture by goading into self-willed effort instead of appealing to our new nature. In the former you'll infuse the words with pre-embedded messages like: "You should be better; try harder to fix yourself; what's wrong with you?" The messages in *The Room of Grace* are quite different: "You are exactly who I have made you to be; what I am describing in these passages are who you now are, and what you are fully longing and able to live out! This is not a set of impossible standards to beat yourself up with. This is what the new you has waited to get to do." God does not speak in contradicting voices, based on how much coffee He's had. He has one voice. He is not schizophrenic. He is the living God. But our interpretations have often been schizophrenic. It's time for such madness to end.

> **Good Intentions appeal to:**
>> the old life
>> striving, independent self-effort
>> conditional acceptance
>> critique and condemnation

> **Grace is all about:**
>> the new life
>> God's ability in you
>> Christ's love
>> settled righteousness

So, here's this chapter's verse:

> ***Without faith it is impossible to please God.*** Hebrews 11:6

This, maybe, is an unfamiliar way of thinking. Anyone who wants to, take a shot at answering this question: Based on its intentions of striving self-effort enablement, how might this verse be emphasized or taught in *The Room of Good Intentions*?

We've wondered in preparing this study, how close your observations would be to ours. So, each time, after you've had a chance to respond, we'd like to take a stab at the same answer. All of our insights together will help us grow in learning to recognize when we're seeing timeless truth through dead filters and replace them with life-giving insight.

So, read out loud our observations of how we imagine many of us have been taught to see such a verse in *The Room of Good Intentions.*

> . . .to stress a need to proving you have enough faith to please Him?

> . . . emphasize all the things you need to do to "seek Him?"

> . . . create a checklist of what's needed to show your faith and prove your devotion?

> . . . be in doubt if you're really pleasing Him and disappointed in your efforts?

> . . . be missing the point of this verse entirely?

Now, several could comment on how you imagine this same verse might be viewed in *The Room of Grace*?

"What if Christ is no longer over there, on the other side of our sin?"

Then, read our observations, listening to hear if our observations start to fit with yours to weave a picture of how God is encouraging us to see this scripture:

> . . . Pleasing is a good motive, it simply cannot be our primary motive or we get trapped in a place of *The Room of Good Intentions* interpretation.

> . . . Pleasing God is the *fruit* of trusting God. Pleasing God is also the *fruit* of godliness, not its *root*!

> . . . God wants our primary motive—our first and last waking thought—to be of trusting Him.

> . . . Nothing in the world pleases Him more! If we trust what He says—including whom He says He has made us to be—this pleases Him.

> . . . If we trust Him with our life choices instead of trusting ourselves, this pleases Him.

> . . . The occupants of *The Room of Grace* get the privilege of experiencing the pleasure of God, because they have pleased God by choosing to trust Him.

We hope these reflections are challenging how some of us have seen scripture through a filter. Reading the Bible accurately is at the heart of how an environment is changed. It changes by the citizens of the culture beginning to see themselves, God and His Word without that appeal to unredeemable flesh. Instead, an appeal to our new nature accomplishes whatever we find in His scriptures. We'll do this with another verse each session. Soon, you'll be asking yourself, in everything you read, "Have I imposed something onto this verse that God never intended? Have I manufactured an attitude, motive or self-condemnation onto this passage that has distorted God's intention?" We're learning how to read the scriptures from *The Room of Grace*. It changes everything.

PART 4: TRYING THIS ON

It's imperative to locate where we're *living right now*. Give anyone who'd like a chance to answer this next question.

Which of these three places best describes where you are currently in your relationship with God?

> *The Room of Good Intentions*
>
> *The Path of Cynical Disillusionment*
>
> *The Room of Grace*

Please read this next piece to each other, even though you'll be doing it alone during the week

PART 5: SETTLING CONVICTIONS

If you are able, find some time alone this week and try to imagine the scenes depicted in the "Two Roads" chapter. Recall how you've experienced God when you've failed at something. **What was His expression? How did you feel in His presence?**

Now try to imagine, right after a failure, experiencing Jesus with His arm around you, whispering, "I know. I've known from before the world began. And I'm not ashamed, I'm not angry. I'm crazy about you. I've got your back. I'm here. I love you."

If it feels uncomfortable to view God this way, ask yourself, "Why?" It might be time to risk believing that what Jesus did on the cross purchased not only heaven, but this scene, this relationship, this unmerited affection. Understanding His love this way is intended to give you permission to trust His love every moment of every day for the rest of your life.

. . . Imagine. Believe. Enjoy. Repeat.

SESSION NOTES

_____

_____

_____

_____

_____

_____

_____

_____

_____

_____

_____

_____

_____

_____

_____

_____

SMALL GROUP PRAYER & PRAISE SHEET

Briefly share your prayer requests as a small group, recording the requests below. Remember to record any answers to prayer below.

PERSON	PRAYER REQUEST	PRAISES/ANSWERED PRAYERS

Welcome back friends! Pick someone to do the reading, get comfortable and let's get back at this. (And to the guy over there on the side, if you're going to make all that noise with those mints, the least you can do is share them with the group.)

PART 1: CINEMA

After watching these clips, take a few minutes to discuss these questions:

1. In the first film piece of the young woman as a mother, a socialite, and businesswoman, what masks do you think this woman is wearing? And why does she wear them?

2. In the running clip titled, *My New Identity*, did you identify with those people in the first half of the piece who were running for mistaken reasons?

PART 2: GROUP

Now, we move deeper into the concepts of the book.

"Nothing is more embarrassing or vulnerable than nakedness. Not knowing another option, we hide ourselves. It wasn't just that Adam and Eve did something wrong. They were both convinced something was now uniquely and terribly wrong about them, with them. This is how shame works, and it's different from guilt. Guilt wants to lead us to forgiveness, to be cleaned. Shame drives us to hide, convinced we cannot truly be forgiven or made clean. It forced them and has forced us to cover ourselves with whatever was available at the time." (*The Cure,* pg. 30)

From what you just read, allow anyone to answer these questions.

1. How is shame different from guilt?

2. Have you ever felt like shame was driving you to wear a particular mask?

3. How does *The Room of Grace* make it possible for people to no longer be driven or identified by their shame?

PART 3: TAKING OFF THE FILTER

In this section, we want to get in touch with the cost of staying in an environment which is focused on pleasing God by our performance. We hide, we posture, we bluff, we fake it, and we put on masks.

We do this because none of us can ultimately measure up to our own standards, let alone the one's we presume God is demanding. So we find a way to drum up something we hope will be enough. We don't believe we are good enough to be loved, to be accepted, and to keep our seat at the table.

We might ask, "Which came first?" The twisted interpretation of scripture that created the lies we tell ourselves, or the lies we tell ourselves creating the twisted interpretation of scripture? It started with the lies we've believed from long before we trusted God. And now we carry those lies into what we presume He'd want to say after we mess things up. So we can create a presumption of His disdain and impatience for us to pull it together on our own, not based on His character, but our shame. So again, let's take a look at scripture. Let's again help each other see the unvarnished Word, without added dead presumptions.

Let love be without hypocrisy. Romans 12:9

OK, once again, whoever would like, answer this: How would you expect this verse to be emphasized and taught in *The Room of Good Intentions*?

Let us add to your thoughts. Read our observations of how we imagine many of us have been taught to see such a verse in *The Room of Good Intentions*.

. . . try to "man-up," and push yourself harder to "walk the talk."

. . . try to "will" yourself into loving people with more sincerity.

. . . avoid conviction by focusing on how others need to be less hypocritical.

Now, a few of you, answer this: How do you think Romans 12:9 might be taught and emphasized in *The Room of Grace*, without the moralistic filter?

Then:

Here's what we think about when we read this without the filter of *The Room of Good Intentions*. In *The Room of Grace* you might read this verse and:

> . . . realize that this love is already in you and doesn't have to be added on.

> . . . decide to relax because Christ is now dwelling in you every moment of every day.

> . . . discover living in this identity frees you from wearing masks and lets you experience and share more.

> . . . stop focusing on sinning less and realize that sinning less doesn't mean loving more. However, loving more will automatically mean sinning less.

> …delight in the reality that hypocrisy vanishes when I no longer have to hide, or bluff or pretend I'm someone I'm supposed to be. It vanishes in the safety of the absolute, unchanging delight of my God and who He says I am.

Maybe we're starting to see how the scriptures are not describing an impossible list that we'll never quite pull off, so we can get right with Him. Instead they're describing the very delightfully doable life of one who is right with Him; fully righteous, fused with God and full of the love that meets the only request He gives. Every time we encourage ourselves to read the scriptures, by trusting the new life in me and letting it be wooed out, we are building this new way of living in Him—together!

"Why would any of us ever put on a mask again?"

PART 4: TRYING THIS ON

"What if there was a place so safe that the worst of me could be known, and I would be loved more, not less, in the telling of it?"
(The Cure, pg. 38)

Take time for anyone who wants to respond to this pretty daunting question.

Q: Do you think it is possible to experience such a safe place? Why or why not?

Please read this next piece to each other, even though you'll be doing it alone during the week.

PART 5: SETTLING CONVICTIONS

It would be great for you to keep asking yourself during this week . . .

1. How does God want me to live out the unique role He has written for me? Is it really His desire that I "be myself?"

2. Why should I try to fool God and others into thinking I'm someone else?

3. If I believe Christ when He says I am righteous and not condemned, is that real and strong enough to keep me from putting on masks?

4. Is there anyone in my life I might risk trusting enough to let them love me more by knowing the real me?

> "And when you reach it, unresolved issues will begin to heal. You'll gather up stacks of masks and toss them in the dumpster, brushing your hands together as you walk away. Then, you'll walk out into the daylight, your skin feeling the morning air for the first time since you can remember. You'll drink in the beauty of flowers and earth, free from those nauseating fumes of epoxy holding your face to a mask."
> *(The Cure*, pg. 38)

SESSION NOTES

SMALL GROUP PRAYER & PRAISE SHEET

Briefly share your prayer requests as a small group, recording the requests below. Remember to record any answers to prayer below.

PERSON	PRAYER REQUEST	PRAISES/ANSWERED PRAYERS

CHAPTER TWO
THREE GODS

No 2.

No 7.

6.

No 12.

No 11.

No 17.

No 16.

Welcome back friends! Pick someone to do the reading, get comfortable and let's get back at this. (This is the third week and still nobody has brought guacamole?)

PART 1: CINEMA

Q: From these pieces, what are you hearing about who God says you are?

PART 2: GROUP

Now, let's move deeper into the book chapter.

We're now at the heart of the journey. Nothing you believe and depend upon is more magnificently liberating than this single truth: You are no longer who you were, even on your worst day. Trusting and leaning upon "Christ in you" is the source of every shred of strength, joy, healing, and peace.

What happened in that first moment of trusting Jesus affects everything. This start is called "justification," which means "to be made right."

The difference between seeing God "OUT THERE" with me striving to become more righteous, and seeing God "IN ME" already fully righteous, is the difference between man-made religion and God-infused life. This truth brings freedom to the captives!

As a group, we need to stop here and wrestle this truth to the ground. Every other hope grows from trusting this reality. Who God says I now am in Him is the basis for how I face sin, how I heal, experience love, mature, and enjoy life! Sadly, many believers don't get this. Their choice not to believe this truth is what breeds striving and cynicism.

"No one told me that when I wear a mask, only my mask receives love."

Stop right here. Answer the first question. Then and only then, go on to the next one. Do not pass Go. Do not collect $200. (Sorry, old Monopoly reference.) So, at least a couple of you, answer this:

1. Before this study, what have you believed about you actually being righteous?

2. If people believe themselves to be actually righteous, why might some religious leaders fear that in their followers?

3. What difference does it make in our approach to life, whether we're trying to change into who we *should be*, or maturing into who we *already are*?

PART 3: TAKING OFF THE FILTER

Remember, there is a way of seeing, awaiting us, in *The Room of Good Intentions* that slants our interpretation of scripture. Those of us who have only read the Bible through this lens get to challenge our assumptions in the light of unfiltered truth.

Here's this week's verse:

> *He made him who knew no sin to be sin on our behalf, so that we might become the righteousness of God in him.* 2 Corinthians 5:21

This is a hugely, pivotal verse that has been often obscured by the filter of man-made religion. So, let's spend some time examining how the wonder of our actual righteousness, expressed in this verse, might get watered down.

This subject is the most daunting of any in the book. So, we'd like to give you our observations first in this chapter, if only to give common language to help you in answering this section yourself.

So read our observations first about how this verse might get taught in *The Room of Good Intentions*.

No 4. \|\|\|\|\|

No 5. \|\|\|\|\|

No 9. \|\|\|\|\|

No 10. \|\|\|\|\|

No 14. \|\|\|\|\|

No 15. \|\|\|\|\|

No.19. \|\|\|\|\|

No 20. \|\|\|\|\|

In *The Room of Good Intentions*, we might:

> . . . presume that Jesus became sin so we would care enough to try and make ourselves more righteous.

> . . . see the word "might" in this verse as implying that some won't quite get to this righteousness.

> . . . believe this righteousness is only legal (theoretical) and not actual.

> . . . read these words as a challenge to be more caring based on all He has done for us.

(We know. This is deep sledding. Hang in there. This is about as important as it gets.)

Now:

Several of you answer this: Do our observations sort of connect with what you were thinking? Which ones? Do you have other observations?

Now, let us do the same with how 2 Corinthians 5:21 can be understood in *The Room of Grace*.

Read our observations. Maybe you've already figured out some of these insights, but humor us anyway. Understanding 2 Corinthians 5:21 *In the Room of Grace,* you might:

> . . . accept the logic of the argument that in the same way Jesus became actual sin, you actually became righteous.

> . . . upon learning the verb "become" is in a tense meaning *once and for all*, you could accept that you became righteous at the moment of trusting Jesus, and not as a progressive *becoming* from self-effort.

> . . . upon discovering the verb carries no question of doubt, you could accept that, because He became sin on our behalf, you became the righteousness of Christ in Him.

No 1. \|||||||
No 2. \|||||||
No 4. \|||||||
No 6. \|||||||
No 7. \|||||||
SLIDE MOVE \|||||| ANDERSON8
FILM ROLL \|||||||
No 8. \|||||||
No 11. \|||||||
No 12. \|||||||
No 13. \|||||||
No 16. \|||||||
No 17. \|||||||
No 20. \|||||||
No 18. \|||||||

Now, any of you, answer this next question:

Do these above insights make sense to you? Take a few minutes together to try these on. We want to come live in your garage and make ourselves available to process these with you until they do make sense. They are that important.

This is new for many of us, to actually consider how our view of God and ourselves has shaped our interpretation of the scriptures and then frustrated how we live out this life. But the freedom, healing, and empowering to be loved and to love, which comes from taking off the moralistic lens, is life-altering.

PART 4: TRYING THIS ON

This section is always about making personal the truth we've been discovering together. This is the place where we start to try on the new coat. Don't rush this.

Most of us have imagined God as "out there, up there, over there" and tried to get more of Him by *doing* something or caring more. It has worn us out and left us with no more than we started with.

Give time for at least someone to answer this question:

1. So, what difference do you imagine it would make if you could believe that you have all of Jesus *right now* because He lives in you, you live in Him, and you are completely righteous in Him?

Please read "Part 5" to each other, even though you'll be doing it alone during the week.

"Soon, I was back to trying to impress a God I imagined was growing more and more impatient with me."

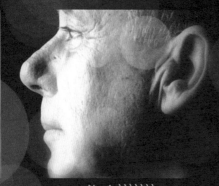

No 4. \\\\\\\

No 5. \\\\\\\

No 9. \\\\\\\

No 10. \\\\\\\

No 14. \\\\\\\

No 15. \\\\\\\

No.19. \\\\\\\

No 20. \\\\\\\

PART 5: SETTLING CONVICTIONS

This isn't just wishful thinking. Here are some great verses to dwell on during the week:

> Philippians 3:9-10. "...not having a righteousness of my own derived from the Law, but that which is through faith in Christ, the *righteousness which comes from God on the basis of faith*."

> Galatians 2:20. "I *have been* crucified with Christ; and it is no longer I who live, *but Christ lives in me*; and the life which I now live in the flesh I live by faith in the Son of God, who loved me and gave Himself up for me."

> 2 Corinthians 5:17. "...if anyone is in Christ, he *is* a new creature..."

Paul says in Philippians 3:10 that he wants to embrace this righteousness and experience Jesus as fully as possible here on earth. He knows if he depends in any measure on his own manufactured righteousness he'll miss intimacy with Christ. How transforming it would be to feel and live the same way!

Finally, if you're up to it, reflect upon the implications of this truth:
> "Your view of you is the greatest commentary on your view of God." (*The Cure*, pg. 44)

See you next time.

"All masks crumble, because they are man-made."

SESSION NOTES

SMALL GROUP PRAYER & PRAISE SHEET

Briefly share your prayer requests as a small group, recording the
requests below. Remember to record any answers to prayer below.

PERSON	PRAYER REQUEST	PRAISES/ANSWERED PRAYERS

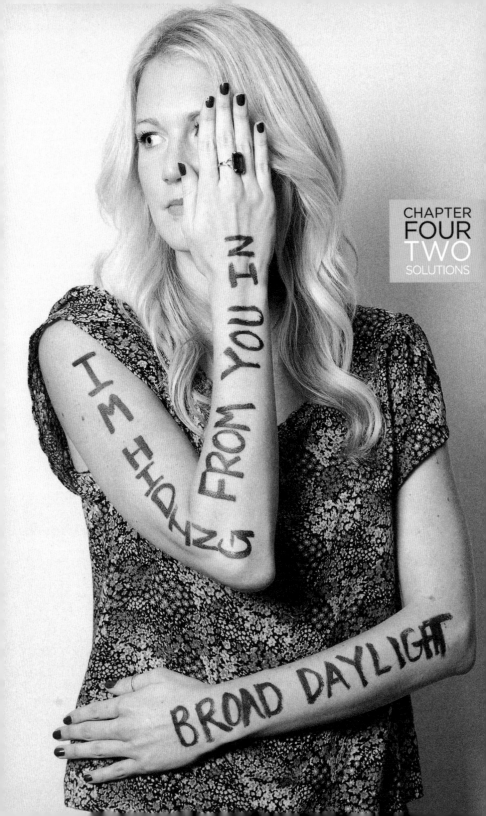

Welcome back friends! Pick someone to do the reading, get comfortable and let's get back at this. (This is week four. Even our own family members haven't made it this far. Congratulations!)

PART 1: CINEMA

Q: What might you write on your arms that would surprise others?

PART 2: GROUP

By now we're getting a sense of the DNA of an environment of grace, so let's start picturing what it looks like in daily life. It's time to consider how an environment of grace would change the way we view our own sins. In *The Room of Good Intentions* we try to control our behavior by self-effort, diligence and intense discipline. But it reveals how much we think of our independent ability to face our sin and how little dependence we place upon God's ability to solve our sin.

How we see God affects how we give ourselves permission to sin. The hostess in *The Room of Grace* said,

> "That's how it starts with me. I see a picture of God 'over there,' indignant and aloof to my heart and my needs, hurts, failures…the wrong that has happened to me. Then I start trying to solve the hurt by myself, but I don't even know the base issues, let alone how to fix them! But that's what I do. I stop believing God is able or even wants to solve my flaws.
>
> "Then I feel sorry for myself, like I'm a victim of God's random acts and lack of protection. This is where the self-entitlement comes in; 'I deserve this. I owe this to myself. God doesn't understand me, or my needs. I don't think He cares fully and He's been holding out on me.
>
> "And now my heart's inflamed, hooked, ready to plot a move."
> (*The Cure, pg. 54*)

Self-protection might be the most absurdly ridiculous two words ever put together.

It is hugely important to understand how sin can be faced and its power broken in *The Room of Grace*. This "control cycle" is not limited to certain forms of sin. Every single one of us runs the course of this control cycle at various times, and in many varied expressions.

Here, below, is a visual depiction of the control cycle the hostess walked us through in *The Cure*. All of the triggers you see here she has walked through in her story. This drawing is an illustration of the course sin will inevitably take unless I tell another. The Gap is the place in my life where I am living with nothing hidden.

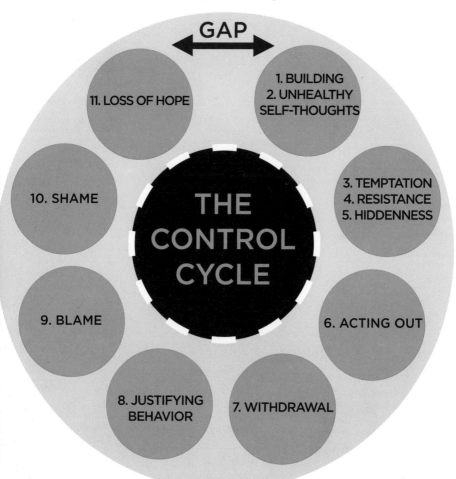

Everyone spend a few moments just examining the components and flow of this cycle.

Then, take some time for a number of you to answer these questions:

1. How do my unhealthy self-thoughts help fuel this control cycle? (Don't go to the next question, until you've taken a stab at this one first.)

2. The power of sin is revealed not when I act out, but in the permission I give myself to act out and not disclose what I'm about to do. Why is it harder for us to admit we're going to do something than it is to admit that I have actually acted out?

3. We say that once this cycle has begun, if at any stage you do not tell another, you will always, inevitably move to the next stage on the cycle? Why?

PART 3: TAKING OFF THE FILTER

We thought we'd take a stab at this verse in James to tie into this chapter.

> *"... confess your sins to one another, and pray for one another, so that you may be healed."* James 5:16

OK, let's get after this again. Anyone, how might this verse get taught poorly in *The Room of Good Intentions*?

Here are our thoughts. Please read aloud where we think the bias would fall in *The Room of Good Intentions*:

You might read "confess your sins to one another, and pray for one another, so that you may be healed" as . . .

> . . . "you'd better or else."

> . . . a magic formula or technique.

> . . . something you do only when you get to the place of really acting out.

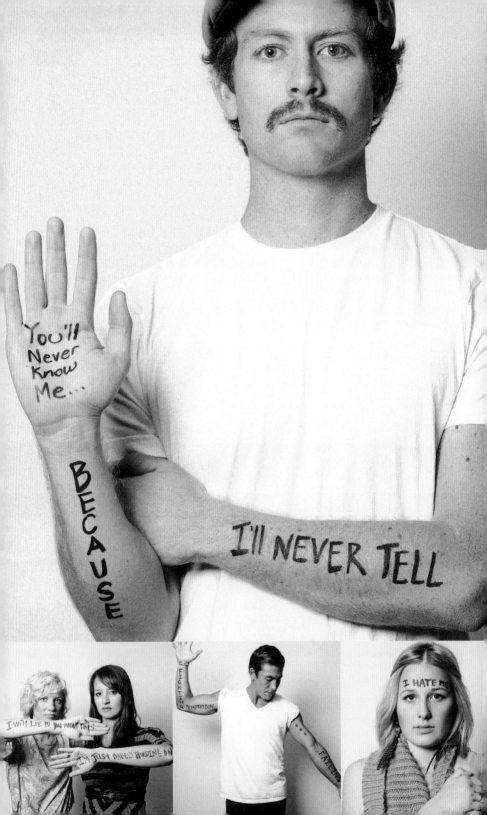

Next, let's hear from one or two about how James 5:16 could be understood in *The Room of Grace.*

Here are some thoughts we had from the verse . . . take some time to consider them aloud.

> . . . Confession puts me in touch with Christ's work for all my junk. It's a priceless gift to have His work take care of my sin because none of my own work can "heal" my sin.

> . . . Confession is an amazing way of receiving God's love through another person.

> . . . Confession heals me from sin issues by letting others into my life so they can love me. Love is one of God's primary healing agents.

> . . . Confession means I risk trusting others who I see as saints who sin; I may respect them as trustworthy, but I know they are not perfect.

> . . . Confession reminds me that I am a child of the light already, and because of this truth I can risk living in the light.

> . . . Confession is an opportunity to call out to others for protection, even when I'm beginning to give myself permission to "go dark" with my sin.

"I stop believing God is able or good enough to solve my flaws."

PART 4: TRYING THIS ON

We've been learning that if at any stage of this cycle I choose not to disclose my intentions to another, the next step is inevitable. But if, at any stage I choose to disclose my intentions, the next step is suddenly avoidable.

Several questions here for any of us to discuss:

1. We say, we're the one person we can't protect? Why is that true?

2. Why do I need you to help protect me?

3. Here's one to ask later, for that person you choose to trust with you before the cycle starts up. "How can I best let you protect me?" This question will be answered over a walk, maybe even with someone after your group meeting ends. Again, this is not a 7-week study. This is our lives.

"'So, I resist for a while.
'I'll talk myself out of this;
I'll resist enough;
I'll stuff it away.'"

Please read this next piece to each other, even though you'll be doing it alone during the week.

PART 5: SETTLING CONVICTIONS

The power of sin is broken in coming out of hiding.

Very few words have as much power or hope as this sentence above.

It is astounding to discover that God has created others to be our way home when we find ourselves trapped in any area of sin. We have been going it alone for so long, trying bravely to buck-up and fight our way through temptation. When we live this way we rarely experience love of others.

We can only be loved when we allow another to meet our needs.

Soak in these two truths this week. Let God direct you into applying them in your present reality. Here's one option: Call the friend you are growing to trust and take him or her out for coffee. Share these truths and your intention to live by them. You'll be giving them part of your life story, just as the hostess shared part of her story in this Chapter Four. Such vulnerability will change and deepen the texture of your friendship and lay the foundation for protection and freedom for the rest of your life.

"Whenever I think I'm in control of sin, it is, in fact, controlling me."

SESSION NOTES

SMALL GROUP PRAYER & PRAISE SHEET

**Briefly share your prayer requests as a small group, recording the
requests below. Remember to record any answers to prayer below.**

PERSON	PRAYER REQUEST	PRAISES/ANSWERED PRAYERS

CHAPTER
FIVE
TWO
HEALINGS

Welcome back friends! Pick someone to do the reading, get comfortable and let's get back at this. (Second thought, we want you to be comfortable, but at least try to sit up!)

PART 1: CINEMA

Q: Talk with each other about how the piece with the anorexic girl affected you or challenged you.

PART 2: GROUP

Please read this:

> Forgiveness breaks down walls, frees hearts, mends countries, restores families, and draws out the best in us. It can turn hatred into tenderness and the desire to destroy into a passion to protect. It is more powerful than any weapon, government, or wealth. Nothing else can bring such profound healing. Forgiveness forms the foundation of our relationship with God and sustains our relationships with each other. When we unleash this gift, by receiving it in humble trust that God can actually free our heart and heal our relationships, then the miraculous can happen. This powerful gift has one purpose: to protect us from the insidious harm that comes from sin done against us.

One of the greatest gifts of living in *The Room of Grace* is the ability to release our grip on being in control and instead trust God's power, love, sovereignty, and faithful protection. Nowhere is this more visibly and profoundly experienced than in the healing reality of forgiveness!

We have tried over and over to forgive another before we've forgiven that person before God. And it never sits right. We say the words, but at the end of the day, we're still carrying the wrong done to us like a dead animal strapped to our backs. This section offers hope and healing we'd almost forgotten existed.

In *The Room of Good Intentions* we try to conjure up a forgiveness out of our own willpower, while still deeply wounded and resentful. It never works. We end up faking a relationship. In *The Room of Grace*, through trust of His ability, we allow God to free us from all those barbed hooks keeping us trapped in our bitterness. This is for our sake, to free us, so we can go to the other in authentic love, for their sake. It is one of the most miraculous healings we get to see in this lifetime—when a human voluntarily gives the pain done to them to the only One who can carry it.

Many of us are pretty fragile and raw in this area. Give the great gift of listening to each other carefully. Incredibly sacred transactions are being considered.

Question:

1. What does it feel like to be inflamed by another's sin against me?

Once you've answered that one, then at least one of you explain this:

2. What does it mean, that before we can forgive a person horizontally for their sake, we must trust God's protection so we can forgive them vertically, for our sake?

(This point is huge. If no one is clear on its answer, go back to the book and read the section on horizontal and vertical forgiveness. Only then go forward. This distinction is the difference between forgiveness that heals and a false forgiveness that doesn't.)

3. What's the distinction between forgiving and trusting an offender? How does blurring these two keep us stuck in unforgiveness?

"We can almost picture God forced to sit on his hands, waiting until we give up so he can rescue us."

PART 3: TAKING OFF THE FILTER

Here's the verse we picked because it ties pretty tightly to this chapter:

> *. . . forgiving each other, just as God in Christ also has forgiven you.* Ephesians 4:32

This is the big ticket item; reflecting on how to see the scriptures without a life-draining filter.

Several of you, please take a stab at answering this: How might you expect this verse tappealingaught in *The Room of Good Intentions*?

Then:

Read our thoughts. You're probably getting so practiced at this that you no longer need us. But still, please, continue to humor us.

In *The Room of Good Intentions*, the emphasis of the verse might be taught as...

> . . . a demand because Christ has forgiven you, instead of seeing the "process" nature of the forgiveness you are to extend.

> . . . meaning "just get over it because Jesus just got over it."

> . . . a method, a mantra, where you quickly try to get past the incident.

Next. Could several answer, how might Ephesians 4:32 be understood in *The Room of Grace*?

Then:

Here are our additional thoughts about forgiveness. Read and react, if you'd like:

> . . . He is appealing to our new hearts to do what the real me now longs to do-be freed and released from my own hurt, so I can love the one who wronged me.

> . . . He is describing the nature of the forgiveness exhibited in Jesus, which my new heart can now emulate, because I have the fused love of Christ fully active in me.

> . . . He is describing how I can trust God with the process of dealing with all the injustice and pain, just as Jesus trusted His Father with the injustice and pain.

> . . . He is describing how I can be freed from my own bitterness by trusting God to be in charge of defending me in the injustice done to me.

PART 4: TRYING THIS ON

The Cure makes some startling statements about repentance.

2 Timothy 2:25 in the *New American Standard* calls repentance a gift. What difference would it make to trust repentance as a gift instead of a striving promise you must somehow, this time, try to keep.

Repentance isn't doing something about my sin. It is instead admitting that I can't do anything about my sin. It is trusting that He alone can, because at the Cross, He died for every sin. He died for every sin because I can't manage, deal with, or stand up to any sin.

Have several answer this:

Q. Is this understanding of repentance different from what you've grown up with?

Please read this next piece to each other, even though you'll be doing it alone during the week.

PART 5: SETTLING CONVICTIONS

It would be astoundingly healing to get alone and examine relationships in your life where you've been harboring unforgiveness or unrepentance.

> "Never is the proof of new life more evident than when I cede control because of my trust in His character, love and power." (*The Cure, pg. 74*)

Reread the book chapter. Then, if and when you're ready, tell God you're tired and weary enough to stop carrying the pain and injustice that's not yours to carry alone, and trust Him with it.

This might be one of the most freeing weeks you'll get to experience in this lifetime. And if you're like many of us, you get your life back.

"The first condition to returning home is we must be weary enough."

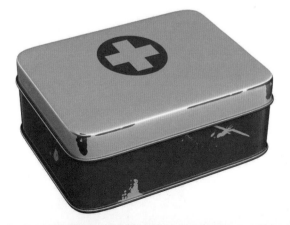

SESSION NOTES

SMALL GROUP PRAYER & PRAISE SHEET

Briefly share your prayer requests as a small group, recording the
requests below. Remember to record any answers to prayer below.

PERSON	PRAYER REQUEST	PRAISES/ANSWERED PRAYERS

Welcome back friends! Pick someone to do the reading, get comfortable and let's get back at this. (By the way, cool videos in this series, huh? Here are some more!)

PART 1: CINEMA

In the second clip, our friend asks, "If I really messed up and really failed, who would I tell?" He discovered he had no one. Over the years he has found a few who he truly feels safe with to express the hardest life issues. Now, they're no longer attempting to solve their life issues by themselves; hiding, covering, bluffing, pretending.

Q: Question: Are many you know without such safe, authentic friends in their lives?

PART 2: GROUP

By now you've read this statement several times: "What if there was a place so safe that the worst of me could be known and I'd discover that I would not be loved less, but actually loved more in the telling of it?" But in *The Room of Good Intentions*, well-meaning friends are trying to help get your *symptoms fixed*. It's often about them not wanting to be embarrassed by your behavior.

The sum effect keeps us on guard, hiding and bluffing. *We must change the DNA of the culture.* We want to be encouraged into relationships of love, where it's *less important that anything gets fixed, than that nothing ever has to be hidden.*

I must ask myself if I care more about getting your issues resolved or establishing a healthy relationship so the issues can be resolved?

In *The Room of Good Intentions*, I make you accountable to me, so I can control your behavior, so you don't embarrass me too much. The result is:
* you end up hiding,
* you resent and mistrust me,
* your unresolved issues remain unresolved and buried alive!

In *The Room of Grace*, I want to earn your trust so you'll want to give me permission to protect you. The result is:

* you end up hiding less and less,
* you trust in the safety of my commitment to you,
* your unresolved issues begin to be resolved and healed because they're in the light!

Please read these aloud, and then, well, you know what to do...

1. What's the difference between attempting to *fix* issues and *resolving* them?

2. Why is it more important to nurture an environment where nothing is hidden than to fabricate one where everything appears neat and fixed, but is hidden?

PART 3: TAKING OFF THE FILTER

"Bear one another's burdens, and thus fulfill the law of Christ." Galatians 6:2

By now we're learning to listen to each other's observations more than react to them. So, let's try another verse.

Have as many as want to share how this might be emphasized or slanted in *The Room of Good Intentions*.

Then:

Read our takes at how Galatians 6:2 might be stressed in *The Room of Good Intentions* by . . .

. . . trying to keep a law by doing enough "bearing" of other's burdens?

. . . being taken as a command to "endure" messed-up people?

. . . being read as another on a long list of things you aren't doing enough of?

Next, share a couple responses of how Galatians 6:2 would probably be taught in *The Room of Grace*.

Then:

Here's ours. Go slowly on these. You could even reflect on them after they're all read. We think they're pretty important.

> . . . this "law" is not the 11th commandment, but an entirely new order of commandment from Jesus. This one your new heart delights to obey.

> . . . this "law" means standing with each other in our hurts, pains, failures, and confusions. It is what Jesus talks about in John 13:34: "A new commandment I give to you, that you love one another, even as I have loved you, that you also love one another."

> . . . this verse gives you an invitation into what most fulfills your new nature. As one who has received love from Jesus and is receiving love from others, you are freed to stand with friends to love them and protect their hearts.

PART 4: TRYING THIS ON

The spiritually immature are not loved well. Not because they fail. They are not loved well because:

* they fail to trust the love of another.
* they trust no one, so their needs don't get met.
* their needs don't get met, so they live out of their selfish wants.

1. (Anyone) If the above is true, what do the spiritually immature need most from us; their parents, teachers, leaders, friends?

"There's a way of seeing God in that room...
Nothing's really been changed in you. Maybe
you get some fairy dust, if you beg hard enough.
But you are basically a not-very-good person
who's trying to be very, very good."

Please read this next piece to each other, even though you'll be doing it alone during the week.

PART 5: SETTLING CONVICTIONS

Make time this week to . . .

Get alone and ask yourself these questions:

Who do I trust to
* Influence me?
* Know some of the hard, vulnerable things about me?
* Receive their love?

Who trusts me to
* Allow me to influence them?
* Know some of the hard, vulnerable things about them?
* Receive my love?

Consider doing this with the people who come to mind :

1. Let those who trust you know how deeply you cherish their trust of you. Restate your commitment to them.

2. Let those you trust know how deeply you need their protective love. Restate your permission to them.

If no names come to mind in answer to these questions, it might cause you to consider calling someone you'd like to have such a relationship with. Invite them for coffee or lunch. Share your hope for such an open and honest relationship and invite them into an area of your life. They'll probably be honored and delighted, and you might be surprised at just how long they've been waiting for such an invitation!

SESSION NOTES

_____

_____

_____

_____

_____

_____

_____

_____

_____

_____

_____

_____

_____

_____

_____

_____

_____

SMALL GROUP PRAYER & PRAISE SHEET

Briefly share your prayer requests as a small group, recording the requests below. Remember to record any answers to prayer below.

PERSON	PRAYER REQUEST	PRAISES/ANSWERED PRAYERS

CHAPTER SEVEN TWO DESTINIES

Welcome back friends! Pick someone to do the reading, get comfortable and let's get back at this. (After you make it through this session you're qualified to teach for us at seminars and conferences, and write our books. Please, get to it. We're getting weary.)

PART 1: CINEMA

Q: Where do you believe you are, right now, on your journey of destiny?

PART 2: GROUP

By now you're discovering that the ultimate goal of learning how to live in *The Room of Grace* has never been just about healing. God's ultimate goal is that we be released into the dreams we've not been able to shake all our lives.

Question, anyone:

Q: How is your destiny categorically greater than your potential?

Now, after reading this next part, a couple of you might answer the question on the next page.

"Some wait for their destiny to drop from the sky, accompanied by angels with swords or trumpets. Or both. They may suffer through a particularly painful season and think, 'This must have happened so God could now move me into the exact, perfect plan He has waited all this time to give me. Hallelujah!'" *(The Cure, pgs. 104-5)*

> *They are waiting more than living, missing the destiny that may already be taking place.*

> or...

> . . . they turn grace into a law by straining to one day believe their identity enough, fearing if they don't get to at least 84% trust, God will deny them His perfect will and they will spend the rest of their days preparing the three-bean salad at church functions.

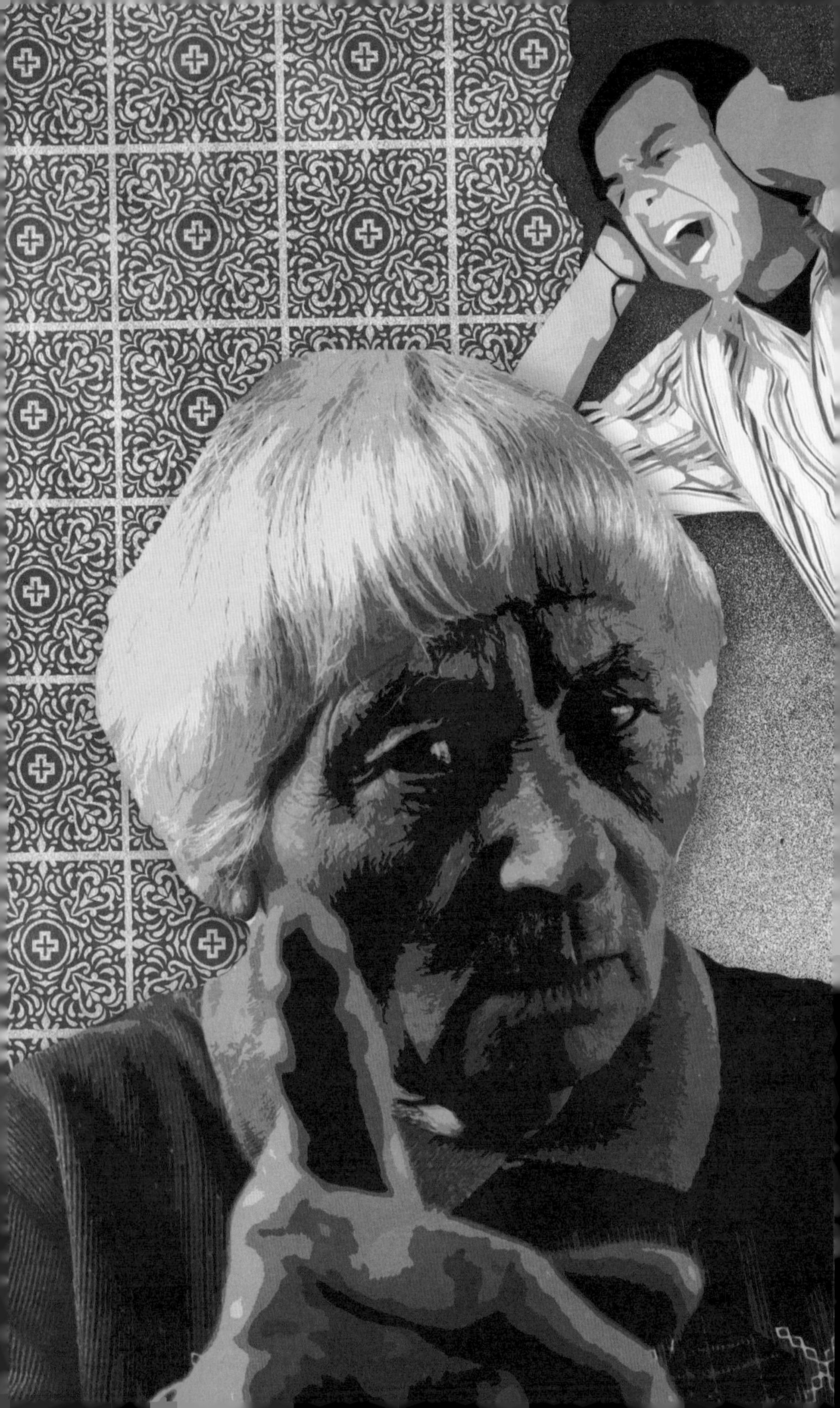

. . . they almost demand it from God, on the basis of how much they've matured, given up, sacrificed, or gone through for Him.

. . . they discount the wonderful destiny God's working in them right now, convinced what they've been given is not significantly dramatic, or profound.

Many miss what greatness looks like to God. It's tempting to think if we have not achieved greatness in number or size it must be because we've not done enough or been enough to warrant His really great stuff. This is a cultural distortion of the gospel. It is distinctly Western and bears the damage of fusing destiny with capitalistic success.

So, here's the question to answer:

Q: Do you think some you know are waiting for a destiny that may be already happening?

PART 3: TAKING OFF THE FILTER

"For we are his workmanship, created in Christ Jesus for good works, which God prepared beforehand, that we should walk in them." Ephesians 2:10

Alright. One last look together at scripture, learning to give ourselves permission to see how God speaks to us: completely righteous believers with new hearts.

So, first, look at this verse carefully. Take some time to ask how would you imagine we would be taught to live this out in *The Room of Good Intentions*?

"I carry these dreams I can't shake. Dreams of the part I *could* play to produce great good."

Then:

Read how we've seen *The Room of Good Intentions* citizens teach this verse.

> . . . as another in a long series of "shoulds" and "oughts" to do more good works.

> ...a command to go find some more things to do. After all Jesus created us for good works!

> . . . "what 'good works' would you be doing right now if you were truly letting God prepare you?"

> . . . as more proof that you aren't walking worthy.

Question for several. What would we hope to pull from Ephesians 2:10 in *The Room of Grace*?

Then:

Here's what we've taught a thousand times from this verse, as we've had the privilege to teach this from *The Room of Grace* . . .

> . . . you don't have to drum up these good works; they've actually been prepared from before the world began.

> . . . you can have the unspeakable joy of awakening each day to walk into a beautiful life of destiny and purpose He's uniquely planned for you!

> . . . you are able to do good works because of who you are now. You have the ability to do what your new heart wants to do!

> . . . you have permission to no longer wait for the perfect situation to arrive, but to see destiny being revealed moment by moment right where you are.

You can do this scripture exercise now with your family, with your friends, your uncle...or the guy behind the counter at the Mexican restaurant down the street. It will yield endless joy, beauty and life. It's the Word of God given the run of our hearts. This is the tone with which God will always speak to those whom He has forever redeemed and given an entirely new heart of love.

PART 4: TRYING THIS ON

God often gives a *mundane-looking* destiny to the most mature. Because only such can trust that around the corner, on a very normal-looking journey, He has some incredibly stunning intention, designed for only you. For the humble, *He will never waste your life or give you a second best destiny*. He has waited for you on this planet from before the world began. He will not bury His intention for you now, even if hurt or loss or fear or failure has convinced you otherwise.

Here's our final request. One by one, try to begin to express what dream or destiny you believe God may be forming, or currently expressing in you. If there's time, it's great beauty for another in the group to affirm that you see a similar destiny forming in them. Enjoy.

PART 5: SETTLING CONVICTIONS

Well, its time to wrap this series up for now. This next section is for you to do during the week. So, before you break up as a group, we wanted to say goodbye. It has been the highest privilege to walk this journey with each of you. Remember, you now have an entire growing library of continuing videos, group exercises and additional writings from us awaiting you in the link at the end of each chapter of the book. Months and months of group or individual time could be spent in each of those chapters. These cinema clips alone will inspire and remind you of where you have been and reorient you when you get confused along this road.

You are not alone. There is a growing community all over the world learning these truths of the Original Good News. We are here. That community is growing. Many of us are on truefaced.com where there are podcasts, blogs, events, testimonies, products, and probably even t-shirts and mugs, for crying out loud!

"Life in *The Room of Grace* teaches us to wait for God's exaltation rather than to pursue position or power."

Stay in touch with us. Follow us on twitter, on our website, on our facebook pages and whenever God brings us nearby your town. Each of us really enjoy pie, just so you know.

Until then, great love in this grace and identity in Jesus . . .

Bruce, Bill & John

Stay in touch with us. Follow us on twitter, on our website, on facebook! Just because we said goodbye, we're not quite done yet. **Please read this next piece to each other, even though you'll be doing it alone during the week.**

In the midst of all the issues facing you, all the disappointment, untied threads, and broken dreams, read and meditate on this statement each day this week:

"The quality of your life is based in trusting this: Where you are right now is the perfect place for you, or the God of all goodness and power would not allow you to be there."
(The Cure, pg. 105)

It is true for all of us that our destiny is:
  ... far greater than our potential!
  ... uniquely and perfectly
      fashioned for us!
  ... too important to compromise!
  ... incredibly worth sticking
      around for!

You are NOT the exception!

You are NOT the one He forgot to give meaningful destiny to!

He is NOT holding out or playing games with you!

___

God created you for purpose. He absolutely adores you. He will have His love lived out through you. For this we were made. This is truly our walk across the stage, our time to represent His heart on earth.

When we get Home, we will see it all revealed in completed wonder. For today, we get to walk out the door and into all the expressions of love customized to all we are from before the world began.

SESSION NOTES

SMALL GROUP PRAYER & PRAISE SHEET

Briefly share your prayer requests as a small group, recording the requests below. Remember to record any answers to prayer below.

PERSON	PRAYER REQUEST	PRAISES/ANSWERED PRAYERS

www.Truefaced.com

Published by CrossSection
940 Calle Negocio #175
San Clemente, CA 92673
800.946.5983
Printed in the USA

First Edition: March 2012

978-0-9847577-3-2 workbook
978-0-9847577-4-9 workbook ebook

VIDEO DEVELOPMENT &
EDITING BY CROSSSECTION:
DOUG MARTINEZ, PRINCIPAL
JASON PEARSON, PRINCIPAL

3 LIVES: REUBEN HERNANDEZ
REUBENHERNANDEZ.COM
CONFESSION: PHOTOGRAPHY BY
MATTHEW MORGAN
MATTHEWMORGAN.NET

VENICE + THE BUS STOPS HERE:
VIDEO BY RYAN RAY

SPECIAL CSV THANKS TO:
KRIS HULL, TAMI HUND, JOHN PEARSON